“We fin [illegible]
on fire [illegible]
Krista’s [illegible]
of the c [illegible]
together [illegible] make change. More than a book, Unearthing Our Roots is a guide for community organizing and solidarity. Want to make change? Read this book!”

— Aleyda Cervantes, poet & social justice advocate

“In Unearthing Our Roots, readers will encounter Krista's powerful and enrolling call to reflect, receive, and act in accordance with our deepest held community values as BIPOC leaders. At once confronting and comforting, Pérez's work holds up a mirror for each of us to view macro and micro forces more clearly, and a lantern to illuminate a path forward to personal, interpersonal and community healing.”

— Julie Davidson, Owner-Operator of Komadre Kombucha & certified Co-Active & Relationship Systems Coach

“Krista Pérez has written a marvel of a book—part memoir, part community organizing guidebook—that will touch and transform many lives. She describes trauma historically experienced by BIPOC and BIWOC communities, then explains how these experiences prohibit us from creating the communities we want to see. Within these pages I hear the scholarship and wisdom of bell hooks, Linda Tuhiwai Smith, and others, but written with the clarity of Pérez's voice and in a language that will speak to younger generations. As she writes in her introduction, 'language is continually evolving to more accurately reflect our truths.' This statement best describes the power and beauty of Unearthing Our Roots."

— Renee Simms, author of *Meet Behind Mars* and professor of African American Studies / Creative Writing

"In Unearthing Our Roots, Pérez took me back to my childhood, reminding me of my family's legacy to serve and the long forgotten gifts bestowed upon me throughout their struggle. This book is a source of healing and strengthening for BIPOC JEDAI and Anti-Racism professionals and practitioners. Thank you, Krista, for your commitment to authenticity, transparency, accountability and sustainability."

— Norinda Rosario Yancey, President & CEO of Fierce Buddha, LLC

Krista R. Pérez

UNEARTHING our ROOTS

Restorative Practices for Cultivating Spaces of Belonging

Contents

Blue Cactus Press and its staff and collaborators work, rest, and reside on traditional territory of the Coast Salish peoples, specifically on land of the Puyallup and Nisqually Tribes. This land was taken under duress via the signing of the Treaty of Medicine Creek in 1854. Since then, it has not been returned to the people it belongs to.

Here, we acknowledge that we benefit and profit from our existence in the South Puget Sound on Puyallup and Nisqually land. We respect and honor these peoples and the land. We also understand this acknowledgement does not replace the work of building relationships or trust–it is merely the first step on our path to doing so.

Here, we give thanks. We raise our hands.

A Note on the Acronyms "BIPOC" & "BIWOC"

Throughout this book, I use "BIPOC" to refer to Black, Indigenous, and People of Color. I use "BIWOC" to refer to Black, Indigenous, and other Women of Color. I feel these acronyms fall short of accurately describing the myriad of experiences we hold as historically excluded and marginalized people. Black, Indigenous, queer and trans communities of color are just a few of the identities held within these acronyms. However, for the sake of shared understanding in this book, and with the recognition that our language is continually evolving to more accurately reflect our truths, I have chosen to use the acronyms BIPOC and BIWOC to refer to the many shared and lived experiences of historically excluded and marginalized people.

I am not claiming to know and understand every individual's experience, nor is it my intent to lump our experiences together. I believe there is nuance and difference in all of our experiences, though what I am hoping to highlight here is the commonality of our innate desire to belong, to heal, and to be in community. I am doing so through my own lens of being. I am a woman of color. I am Mexican-American (I am a proud Mexican woman, though I know and fight back against the homophobia, anti-Blackness, anti-indigeneity, classism, and machismo that is deeply rooted in our culture). I am the daughter of an immigrant and a migrant working mother. I am a mother to two biracial children.

I am writing from the deep desire to heal in community, especially those wounds I have carried with me due to the not-so-beautiful parts of my ethnic culture mentioned above. I do not claim to know any one truth, except for the truth of my own lived experiences that I humbly offer as something to learn from, and to add to the rich troves of experience that so many have shared through writing, song, and teaching. Thank you for letting me share. Thank you for supporting me. Thank you for holding space for me.

I write because I am a healer. My heart, my hands, my words seek to heal. They will pull and push at you until you are examining the very core of who you are; until you are speaking aloud to yourself, your inner child, your lost self, your hurt self, your vulnerable self; until you are soothing yourself; until you are heartbreakingly and soul wrenchingly honest with yourself and others. All to heal you, to nurture you, to become your own home.

What would happen if we became safe homes for ourselves? How might the energy in our physical homes evolve? How might our families change? How might our communities adapt?

Close your eyes. Imagine your home. It does not matter if this is where you currently live. Just imagine the place where you *feel* most at home. Write down every single thing that cultivates that feeling of acceptance, belonging, safety, and ease.

Introduction

Healing our communities means realizing communities are macrocosms of our families and homes. Healing in historically excluded and marginalized communities will not occur despite how much performative work we do for them or how much money we throw at them. Oftentimes, our performative action is used as a band aid. It tells folks, "Hey I tried! I want to include you!" But that is not a long-term investment, nor sustainable. Performative, inauthentic work is only temporary and it leads to performative behavior and tokenization. This, in turn, leads to historically excluded and marginalized communities feeling disenfranchised, lied to, and hurt. This is the opposite of healing. Performative, inauthentic work is not what BIPOC communities need. Historically excluded and marginalized communities need to see real, valuable (or centered) commitment, and do the kind of work that will not leave us when the future seems bleak. We need people to mean what they say, otherwise don't even start the work.

This book is not for White folks. It is not for those wondering how they can connect with their spouse who identifies as a Person of Color (PoC). This book is for the folks in the trenches with their historically excluded and marginalized communities. This book is for those of us who have suffered abuse, loss, pain, and a constant sense of impostor syndrome. It is for those of us who lack representation or the skills to navigate the highs and lows of life. Is this book the answer to those troubles? No, it never will be. Is this book a space to commiserate? Maybe a little. But mostly, this book offers a space that explores what it takes to truly heal our communities.

This work is not for the weak, nor for those who will walk away. This work is for folks who have dug their heels in and are determined to change the course of their lives, families, and communities. This is for those who came to break their chains and heal. This book is for those who need the healing power of community. Those who need to experience the magic of coming together in spaces where we feel safe to let their guard down, stop code-switching, and share, laugh, and commiserate. We historically excluded and marginalized people need spaces in which we can be in community together, hold discussions, have disagreements, and resolve conflict. We also need access to tools and structures that assist us in doing all this safely.

It's time to finally heal our communities. Healing requires a period of time for individuals and the collective to develop processes—time to simply "be" amongst each other, and to feel a sense of cohesion before we can lean toward healing, belonging, and building community.

When I ponder healing in the context of healing ourselves and our communities, so many questions float to the surface of my mind. How can we heal IN community? Can we resolve the guardedness and cynicism so many of us feel by leaning into the sometimes uncomfortable work of healing and building community together? Can we commit to holding space for each other despite our cultural differences, lived experiences, and beliefs? How do we address the trauma we've experienced—which is valid—enough to lean into the proposition that there is, in fact, a way through these difficult, traumatic, and painful experiences, and move into spaces of healing, belonging, and abundance? How do we convince ourselves that we don't have to live in a fragmented space where survival and a sense of thriving are lightyears apart? Can we accept that there is a place of restoration for us? Can we really accomplish this? Does this kind of restorative space truly exist?

I believe so. I believe that in the moments when we are confronted with words, concepts, or ideas that challenge us, or perhaps trigger us, we can allow our hearts and minds to build bridges instead of walls. We can respond to these moments of intense feeling by embracing one another and choosing to hold space with and for each other.

Our community work must stem from a genuine, personal commitment to undoing the systems of oppression that historically excluded and marginalized people experience, as well as a commitment to long-term community and relationship building. We must grab our machetes and put an end to performative behavior. All of us. We must stop giving our word, only to let folks down when we don't follow through. We must lean into the vulnerability of showing up as we are, but showing up, nonetheless. We must personally begin to challenge the idea that if our communities are struggling or something fails within them, then the endeavor is worthless. This is simply not true.

Consider how commitment and investment in our communities can change the trajectory of our collective BIPOC experiences. Imagine what it would look like to show up amongst one another authentically, and to show up with dedication and commitment to the work instead of giving up on one another or our communities. This work may look like building or mending relationships, or whatever your community needs at a particular moment in time. It is amazing what dedication can do. When we pour authenticity and dedication over human beings, they flourish. Nurturing like this may be something as simple as being a person of your word.

This necessary work begins with yourself. Stepping into the spaces in a community where you wish you could show up as yourself or find connection, or find healing, begins with facing your reflection and doing personal work. That journey begins with each of us leading the way, examining how we impact spaces, and investigating how we can help nurture that which we wish to find in these spaces. This is why I always say our communities are a macrocosm of our homes and we, as individuals, are a microcosm. We must do the internal work of investigating the "whys" behind our personal behaviors and our detachment from our communities. For example, I have seen that my commitment to showing up authentically directly translates into relationship building in my personal and community spheres, which is consistent and aligns with who I am and where I want to go. Why? Because I am showing up as I am, which encourages and allows others to show up as they are. It is easier to align with what is meant for us when we commit to showing up authentically. Similarly, I have learned that when I avoid transparency and vulnerability, I find myself lacking in connection. Folks cannot read my mind. Folks can not possibly know what I need without me intentionally choosing to show up in vulnerability and transparency.

These examples are meant to encourage you to reflect upon what you invite into your life, to block what you do not want to invite, and to co-create the community you want to see. When we become proficient, or at the very least comfortable with investigating these questions, we must then pose them to our communities.

It's time to get real with ourselves and with one another. It's time to stop blaming each other for the failings within our communities. It's time for us to heal our relationships and build community together by lifting the weight of misunderstandings, lack of acceptance, and lack of belonging.

My own story begins with my experience as a second grader, when I was told I did not belong. I was told I needed to pick sides, to choose only one friend because it had been decided by others that I was simply not friendship material. I was found unacceptable as a friend because of the color of my skin and my ethnicity. I was devastated. I realized I was different from others. I felt clunky, awkward, ugly, and unwanted. I felt I did not belong, that I had never belonged, that I would never belong. Looking around me, I found no one to validate me or my feelings.

As I grew older, I carried the shame of not belonging. I thought not belonging was somehow my fault. I stopped speaking Spanish for fear that doing so would only further reinforce what I believed was fact: that this place was not for me. That I was not for this place. *That there was no place for me.*

That sense of never belonging compounded over time. Nothing ever fit me. Not clothes, friends, nor my place in the physical world. I felt like I was wearing an itchy shirt: bunched up in some places, too tight in others, and hanging awkwardly on my body. Years passed by and because no one in my family ever named these differences, I couldn't quite put my finger on why I was so different from the children in my classes and so many of our community members.

Now, I know what made me different was, and is, the juxtaposition of my Christian American behavior and expectations with my Catholic Mexican values. It is my Mexican American experience laced with the metaphysical, the whisper of mystery that I can never quite hold but know exists. It was and is my visceral drive for survival and my simultaneous yearning for rest, ease, and luxury.

My experience has always been that I am caught between what I was told is my birthright and what has been my experience since birth. As People of Color, many of us are told stories of who we are, where we come from, and what we can expect. On occasion, our elders or peers will tell us we deserve more, that we belong here, and that everything we dream of can be ours. But we are grounded by the reality of being ourselves, by walking through this world with our skin, language, and any other identifier that says, *I don't belong here.*

It wasn't until I started being in community with other historically excluded and marginalized people that I realized that experiencing my trauma and witnessing trauma take hold of everyone around me was a shared experience. Of course, our traumatic experiences are different, but we were all constantly working through them and doing so in ways I didn't see happening among non-BIPOC identifying people around me, especially when I was young. Yet, it wasn't the trauma bonding us together. It was that every day, we choose to stand in joy, not oppression or suffering. The joy we deliberately choose can weave the spiritual, the physical, and the unbearable together.

Outside of those BIPOC spaces, I sensed that no matter what I did, I would never belong. No matter how carefully I twisted myself into smaller clothes, drab colors, or airless spaces, those spaces were not for me, and I wasn't for them. Somehow, the world wasn't for me and I wasn't for it. Even though I'd learned to breathe when there was no air left, this world still wouldn't accept me. I still wasn't doing quite enough to make this place a "perfect fit." I wasn't accommodating enough, I didn't speak softly enough, and I got too fired up when I spoke. I showed up so unapologetically that folks got uncomfortable in my presence. Even something as simple as my switching to speaking Spanish to accommodate non-English speakers in some spaces makes some White people uncomfortable.

The sense of tension I felt at that time in my life, in those spaces, silently affirmed that I just didn't quite fit. So I left everyone and everything behind. I went where I had always belonged, where I had always fit, where there was always enough air for me to breathe. I went to stories, information, books . . . all of which held space for me to be anyone I wanted to be, to rest, to have ease and luxury. There, in those books, I crafted a beautiful world made up of all of the healing parts of life: the medicinal quality of food and how we cure ourselves with it every day; medicine from the earth, including herbs, tinctures, and teas to access the metaphysical; food as an emotional salve. I was self-healing using anything I could find. I longed to feel my deep-rooted, ancestral culture like this.

There are small things I miss from my youth, like the smell of the herbal tea my grandmother used to make to soothe my stomach, or the dish she cooked every time we visited. The *corridos* my grandfather played as he sat under the tree in his backyard with a cold Budweiser in hand, enjoying the sun and breeze on his face. During the hardest times in my life, it was books and stories, including my own, that took me away and made me feel like I belonged someplace.

As I became a young adult, and then a small business owner at the age of nineteen, I learned the power of building community through food and common experience. I became a mobile kitchen owner. La Estrella Del Norte, where my family and I served Mexican street food made from scratch, was the first taco truck in Kalispell, Montana. I was the cook, the "taco lady," and my mother made handmade flour tortillas, salsas, and served our customers. My five-year-old little sister would husk the tomatillos, refill the condiments, and wipe down the tables. You better believe she got tips! We were known for running La Estrella Del Norte as a family, for bartering with our tamales, and for making custom orders for our regulars. Owning La Estrella Del Norte was what I consider my first taste of cultivating and being in community.

All the stories and information I collected over the years—some through books, but most from those around me—finally began to come together. The sifting I'd always felt inside myself throughout my entire life finally began to settle. The momentum of learning familial recipes and cooking, tasting, serving, and refining those recipes created its own soothing rhythm for me. I began to find a path through the painful experiences of never belonging. I felt like I was finding space for myself; finally, my own life.

The patrons of La Estrella Del Norte began a weekly tradition of coming to eat on the weekends, chatting, and resting. There we were, over two thousand miles from "home," living in community. People would come to order tacos, homemade flour tortillas, salsa, and, sometimes during Christmas, tamales. We would sit outside and share stories that helped us shed the roughness of the ill-fitting armor we'd put on. The armor that, while inadequate, carried us through moments of pain and sorrow. We could marvel at how small the world is when we shared stories. We remembered certain towns together, or certain beaches. We found out we had family from the same towns. We compared recipes and disagreed about which were better. (Comparing recipes was a bit competitive, especially for *Tapatias* like me. It is hard to beat a *Tapatia*, aka someone from Guadalajara, in cooking. Even though I wasn't born there, because my family is from the area, I am considered a *Tapatia*, too! Folks from Guadalajara believe our food is the absolute best, especially our street food.) Our conversations were about the small things, like what kind of cheese to use, the names of places we knew, our grandmother's *mole* . . . These conversations made me feel like I was home. We all did, even if only for a moment.

My story began to take shape before my eyes. The paragraphs began to fill themselves—meaning formed from my thoughts. Words filled the cavernous spaces within me that used to be filled with nothing but hard feelings, longing, and desire. Words, both heavy and light, rendered my heavy emotions weightless. I began to make sense of my life.

I began to understand how much of my life had been impacted by the experiences of my immigrant father and my migrant working mother. I discovered that the addiction I'd witnessed in my grandfather was less that and more an affliction caused by the unfairness of working an entire life in service of someone else's family, with nothing to show for it. My grandfather had worked for years for a farmer as a caretaker of the land (as well as my grandmother, aunts, and uncles when they could). My grandfather's body showed years of wear. The work had taken a toll on him. My grandfather worked with the understanding that he would earn a piece of land in return, as was customary for migrant workers who became caretakers of a farmer's land. In return for toiling, day after day, year after year, folks typically received a piece of land. But my grandfather did not. We witnessed him go into an all-consuming, life-numbing depression for years, until he was not healthy enough to walk anymore. Alcoholism had always been a vice, but paired with the depression, it threatened to cut his life short.

Observing this as a child-turned-adult, when I learned to put words to my feelings and what I was seeing, I was filled with nothing but compassion and understanding for my grandfather and others. I began to understand that our experiences are far more complex than right or wrong, or acceptable and unacceptable. What can we say, really, when we see someone doing what it takes to survive?

Looking around me, I saw stories rising like wisps of smoke above the people I loved. The stories were visible and almost tangible. I saw less of the person they had settled into being and more of the evermoving nuances of their character, the complex nature of what it means to just "be." And I saw that just as I felt the yearning to belong, to be, to love, to rest, so did they. The wings that would carry me through the next ten years of my life were unknowingly forming in those moments of realization. They were ready to carry me further than I had ever imagined I could go.

Fast forward to 2019. Doors kept closing around me. I applied here, interviewed there, but nothing worked out. I'd always been too loud, too blunt, too round, too strong, too smart . . . or maybe just not the right kind of smart. I was always too much of everything but not enough of something. There was, and is, a raw unease in knowing that while I was born here in the US, the color of my skin and my native language tell on me, revealing I am a different version of "American" than other people. Yet, my family's country of origin did not claim me either. So, who was I? Who am I? An American who doesn't belong? An English speaker who hides their second language? An immigrant's daughter who consistently overachieves to prove her worth, yet is still found unworthy or not quite enough?

This song of not belonging and having no home became old and worn out. The record started to skip from being listened to so many times. Then, once after it skipped, I threw it away and wondered why I'd bothered listening to it for so long. It had brought me comfort; it had provided companionship; and at times, this record—with the same lonely songs—had been my only friend. The song served its purpose. It kept me warm on many nights and protected me through many harsh winters. It taught me that I belong nowhere and everywhere at once—that I am ever changing, evolving, and leaning more into who I am, rather than who I thought I was. What is the distinction between who I am and who I think I am? It is the distance between what I've been told, what I've believed, and what I've allowed myself to be. Allowing and belonging. A lifelong journey.

When I moved to Tacoma, I realized I'd been carrying around that broken, scratched record that I didn't need anymore even though I thought I'd thrown it away. Tacoma felt like home. The people here felt like summer. I was finally home. So when I am asked, *how did you conceive of and found the Tacoma Women of Color Collective, The Community Market, and your consulting business*?, I don't think of words as much as I am overcome with emotion. I hold those old feelings of loneliness, of squeezing into tight spaces, the sick feeling of not being heard—like I'm standing at the bottom of an empty well screaming for someone to hear me—and I am overcome with the longing for comfort that feels like family, to see our people be soft, feel joy, and experience life together.

When I began the journey of founding and co-founding these organizations and businesses, I knew there had to be others who felt the same way. And my hunch was right. They were waiting to be seen, to be heard, to confirm what they had been wishing for.

Rewinding back to those three years of serving homemade Mexican street food and watching folks come together to be in community, some locals, many of them visitors, made one thing very clear: everyone is seeking a sense of belonging. Our communities provide that. Community and belonging can be found in almost any space with the right components. We see this evident in bars, clubs, community centers, churches, support groups, online forums . . . the list goes on. Specifically, for communities of color, this seeking to belong is prominent because there are so many spaces where we do not belong. There are so many spaces that are not for us or not created with us in mind. But now, you will see us building our own safe spaces where we feel like we belong.

> **This book is meant to explore what it means to belong; what it means to be in community; how community can be a salve, and to encourage historically excluded and marginalized people to lean into building community.**

You will find reflection and discussion prompts at the end of each chapter. I hope the prompts encourage you to reimagine your relationship with yourselves and others and your community spaces. You will find that most of the content in this book explores the following questions, in one way or another, and at times presents ideas, thoughts, and lived experiences that support the notion that we can, in fact, heal in community. Your first prompt is on the next page.

Reflection & Discussion Prompts for Restorative Circles

- How do we heal ourselves?
- How do we heal our communities?
- What does it mean to heal in community?

CHAPTER 1

Healing Ourselves

Being in community is closely linked to feeling a sense of belonging. When we talk about not belonging, or not fitting in, we are talking about having those feelings within community spaces. When we seek to belong, we are not talking about moments we spend alone. We are talking about the moments when we are surrounded by others, most often those who exist within our homes or communities. We need to feel a sense of belonging there, to be in community with others, to feel invested-in and appreciated.

Recognizing a Lack of Belonging

For communities of color, the lack of safe spaces, or spaces to join in community, has left many of us with a lingering, underlying pain. It is a pain that stems from feeling like we don't belong. We yearn for comfort, familiarity, and often, solidarity. This feeling has left many of us alone, choosing options like working endless hours, sitting at home, lacking companionship or anyone to share the moment with, and drinking and smoking to soften the ache for belonging and togetherness.

These lonely moments have left us wondering, *where is home, really, and where do I truly belong*? We attend new churches, maybe respond to a friendly invitation from an acquaintance, or take on new hobbies in hopes that we can soothe the loneliness. But there is always something missing, be it shared language, experiences held in common, knowing and understanding what it means to walk through this world as a Black or Brown person, as an "other." This often occurs in non-BIPOC settings, in which we yearn to be amongst our own people, where we feel belonging. The experience of being *othered* is like always being the third wheel, or like being part of a circus, where we are looked at for entertainment rather than being engaged with. Being *other* is being the odd one out, the exception and not the standard. It's similar to being looked at like you walked into the wrong room, or someone asking, "Are you lost?" It's being reminded, daily, that this space is not for you and to be in it, you must remember your manners and behave. Being *othered* is rooted in basing the standard on white supremacy, where being white IS the standard, and being Black, Brown, an immigrant who speaks a different language, queer, or at any other intersection within the historically excluded and marginalized community, is all *other*. And when you have skin like ours, hair like ours, or a native tongue like ours, you will NEVER be mistaken for a white person, a person who does not challenge the white supremacist standard by simply being. So where does that leave us in those spaces? Who are we in those spaces? Simply put, we are the *other*.

So we adapt and learn to live with a lack of understanding, a yearning to be amongst folks like ourselves. We learn to live without a sense of belonging, rest, joy, or a sense of being carefree. Instead, we live with a hypervigilance and unattainable standards.

What has being *othered* pushed me into? It has led me to being overworked and on a hamster wheel, proving my exceptionality and forcing myself to stay in survival mode. Like others, I have straightened my hair, bleached it, stayed out of the sun, learned proper English, and chosen my clothes carefully, all to try and meet an impossible standard. But I—we—never do. The catch is that no matter how hard we try, we will never achieve it. That is why we must build our own tables, rooms, and buildings. We must dream, imagine, and create spaces where WE are the standard. WE must become the norm.

Shame and Shadow Work

Shame and shadow work begins with carrying the shame of not fitting in or belonging. We internalize that feeling and pick ourselves apart, wondering, *why? Was it what I shared, or perhaps the way I shared it? Did I talk too loud? Should I not have tried so hard to relate?*

When spending the majority of your life *othered*, we build a filter our words and expressions pass through, a switch that checks us and ensures we don't get too real or comfortable. We conduct a constant self-check, making sure we don't reveal too much for fear of being *othered* even further. And so much of the experience as the *other* are built around acceptance and belonging. We wonder, will we belong if we share our truth? Will we belong if we fail? Will we belong if we succeed? Oftentimes, I think shame shows up in a community setting as a symptom of impostor syndrome.

Recently, I found a certain level of success which I have been working toward for fifteen years now. I deem success as being able to spend more time around my children, getting to relish in their newness and softness, and being a part of their experience here on earth, and them a part of mine. Success, to me, is to be able to work within my community: holding space, sharing resources, amplifying voices, and building community.

Yet I found myself hitting an inexplicable wall of shame recently as well. I sat with it. I investigated the shame and intense feeling of not belonging. Feelings of fraudulence came up. Then, I observed in myself a feeling of owing my work to those around me. I could not own my success. I felt like an imposter. As the truth began to creep back in (that I was in fact deserving of everything I had achieved), I became overwhelmed with emotion and a sense of desperation. I was filled with fear. *But fear of what?* It was fear of losing friends and supporters, and letting myself down. I was afraid of waking up one day to find I couldn't actually do what I said I could do. I felt ashamed of taking ownership of my recognition and success. I kept trying to pawn it off and give someone else the credit. But then I realized that dealing with my shame, my feelings of not belonging, and fear were all my shadow work. I had revealed what I felt were my most vulnerable, pathetic, sad, and fearful parts of myself to *myself*. These were parts of myself that I ran from daily. I hid from them, hoping they wouldn't find me.

> **Shadow work is sitting with the feelings or things we have been running from our entire lives. What those things are varies from one person to the next, though sometimes, there are similarities.**

Investigation is one of the most important aspects of shadow work. If we can sit with ourselves and look at our own face and ask ourselves questions outright, we can begin to see the root of that which we fight against day after day. We finally give those feelings bubbling under the surface the attention they need. We take a good look at the not-so-beautiful parts of ourselves and acknowledge that it is all ok, we are still ok. But we cannot just leave it at that. Doing shadow work is dismantling that which no longer serves us or our purpose. And honestly, nothing else works. Sitting with myself, looking at myself with eyes of compassion and asking, *What is going on?,* is the only thing that will bring about resolution. Releasing the harsh eyes of judgment we so often choose over self-love and compassion is the only way.

When I finally give in and choose self-love and compassion over judgment, I feel relief. I let feelings of shame, guilt, and fear wash over me in waves of tears until the ocean becomes calm again. I face myself squarely. I own every bit of success I have ever achieved. Even if I am afraid, I own it.

But how does my personal lack of belonging, feelings of shame, and consistent othering relate to BIPOC communities? It's simple: when we are perpetually in patterns of shame and lack the sense of belonging we so need to thrive, as a survival mechanism, we detach. We detach from the pain that almost always comes with this lack of belonging. *The pain edges clouds of shame. It's all too painful to bear.* So we disassociate. If we were quiet enough, smart enough, skinny enough, witty enough, professional enough, if we would just charge less, if we just handled things, we would belong, right? Why can't we just do it? Because we long to rest in real belonging. We crave the full satisfaction of belonging: the feeling of a perfect day in which indulgence is a practice along with ease. The terrible feeling of not belonging will have left us.

As members of the historically excluded and marginalized community, I urge us to explore and investigate these potholes of shame and lack of belonging. I urge us to fill up those potholes, mend them, and smooth them over so we can continue on our journey, and step into the ease, rest, and abundance that belongs to us.

A word on self-sabotage, one of the many potholes we hit in this journey: I have found that choosing a mental health day and rest takes power away from self-sabotage. Self-sabotage can look like impostor syndrome rearing its ugly head, and all of a sudden we are quitting a project we started because we feel like we are not good enough to be doing it, or that somehow we tricked folks into trusting us with this work. Self-sabotage can also look like never sharing our whole story. It can be anything we let keep us from being our most real and best selves. When I realized my legacy would not be built in one day, week, or even year, I started to say,

> **I need a rest day.**
>
> **I deserve a rest day.**
>
> **I owe it to myself to not self-sabotage.**
>
> **I deserve to tend to myself as carefully and tenderly as I do everyone else.**

Another serious point of impact is that of the violence that BIPOC communities experience. What is violence in this context and how do we experience violence in community? While this is a deeper topic that deserves its own book, I would be remiss if I did not acknowledge this type of violence, which is invisible yet so common that we've all felt it.

Violence is telling someone to shove down their experiences and who they are. Telling a member of the BIPOC community their *lived* experiences aren't valid is violence. Forgetting missing and murdered Indigenous women while we search high and low for missing white women is violence. Choosing ignorance, apathy, and division in the face of tragedy and brokenness in BIPOC communities is violence. When our people are killed disproportionately in this county and you say nothing, or debate the validity of this, you are committing violence. When a woman of color shares how you or someone else has silenced and undermined her in the workplace, when you gaslight her, you are committing violence. Violence is one hundred tiny tears, sharp blades at the threads holding our communities together.

Shame is the way our daddies treated us
The way our mamas whipped us with their words
The way our brothers beheld us like fragile glass while also despising us
Our sisters needing us to be the savior, someone to crucify, and failing them
Shame is never living up to everyone's need for you to be the one
The perfect one
The one with all of the answers
The one who will suffer for as long as it takes
The one with never-ending love
Shame is being too loud
Feeling too strongly
Being too heavy
Heavy in love
Heavy in loyalty
Heavy in innocence
Heavy in pleasure
Lust
Joy
Indulgence
Shame is being the nun and the lover
The unspoken
I must be both
Shame is carrying it all and never being enough

Commitment to Healing

The more I commit myself to community work, the more the need for internal work becomes highlighted. To show up authentically and in vulnerability for myself, my family, and my community, I must consistently investigate my intentions and purpose. Building community, intention, and authenticity is unlike any other process I know of. It requires ongoing internal work from us. Each component of community building is prefaced by the desire to remove barriers and silos and replace them with access, resources, and bridges that connect us in our experiences, knowledge, and common needs. I believe we can all commit to this process of healing together in community based on this shared desire to belong and stand in community.

Reflection Prompts

- What internal work have you done and how is it linked to your community-building process?
- How can you do our own personal work and simultaneously be in community?

CHAPTER 2

What Does It Mean to Honor Someone?

How many times have you felt awful sharing the pain and loss of your struggles, knowing damn well how hard your mama or dad worked to make a life for you, to make things easy for you? No matter how much they toiled, their efforts didn't erase the way life cut you. Change is born out of this recognition, coupled with moments when you stand up, look around, and say, "I need more than this." There is no shame in saying or wanting that. Say it, shit, scream it if you need to. But then get ready to work.

There is also something to be said about wanting to *do* better, while honoring those who came before you. Those who came before you paved the way for everyone else. It is their shoulders we stand on. Their trials and tribulations have built the foundation for the house we walk through today. Perhaps not all the rooms in that house are in great condition, some of the walls might even be missing, but the foundation? That foundation exists because of those who came before you.

Do Your Research

We begin the work of honoring those that came before us first and foremost by doing research. Look around to see who has been doing the work you want to do in the community. Who has been actively committed to that work long before you came around? Find a way to learn about these folks, whether past or present, and then find ways to collaborate and honor them.

Recently, I have noticed folks collaborating more and starting new organizations, groups, and nonprofits in efforts to bring others together and form community. While it may be true that there is, in fact, a need for community, and that these new organizations are proof of a collective awakening to our need for one another, I often see crucial pieces missing from the start-up of many of these organizations. They are missing elements essential for sustainability. This lack of sustainability thrives without commitment to authenticity, transparency, accountability and without a commitment to seeing the building of our communities through. Often, these groups, agencies, and organizations close or break apart within a year, failing on the commitment they made to themselves, their members, and their community. The reasons vary depending on their intended purpose.

One of the essential elements of building a sustainable organization is conducting proper research. Often, we do not do the research we need to in order to recognize if anyone has already attempted the same feat, or to understand if and how someone may have partially completed the work already. There is no need to reinvent the wheel or start over.

Now, it may be that someone—potentially you—feels they can do a better job. And maybe that is true. But how can we call on our community to support us when we have not supported them, not sought ways to collaborate with already existing efforts? Without this proper groundwork, we cannot foster a strong community-building approach with the necessary components of sustained success. Those components are:

- Buy-in, or individual investment from other community members

- Personal commitment to the process
- Personal framework for accountability

The single most important indicator that the above components are lacking in your community building is a lack of trust. Relationships and community building require trust. Without paying suitable attention to laying groundwork, we will find it difficult to garner the trust necessary to make progress or allow movements to take root. Laying the proper groundwork and doing our research looks like:

- Participating in spaces you desire to build community in. Looking for and attending any events or forums relevant to the space you want to be in.
- Observing and educating yourself on the history of those spaces and the particular community who inhabits it, without placing the burden of education on the folks already in that space.
- Asking folks who have been doing work similar to what you'd like to do if they are willing to connect you with your desired community, especially if you don't know the new community yet.

- Formulate a clear idea about what it is you want to accomplish, then ask local folks for honest feedback about it. This will help you gauge initial responses to your work.
- Do not break the first golden rule of community building.

GOLDEN RULE OF COMMUNITY BUILDING #1: Never, and I mean *never*, assume you know what a community needs better than the people within it.

Now that we've identified how to address adjacent work and folks in a community or network who have similar missions, let's talk about honoring our elders and honoring those who have come before us. Let us ponder what it means to seek-out our elders, honor them, heed their wisdom, and court their blessings along our personal journeys.

Seeking & Identifying Elders

When we work in the realm of building community, we find there are folks along the way who have been pillars of the community, or kin keepers. They are folks who have been investing in, supporting, cooking for, loving on, and fighting with and for our communities for many years. Many times, those people are our elders. They have cooked for the potluck for thirty years. They gathered our families in joy and in mourning. They spent necessary years protesting and marching. Our communities have been kept and maintained by these folks. Our communities have been held together with their sheer willpower and love alone, for many years, and they have not been acknowledged or honored for that work. And perhaps there are also folks and organizations who have been doing the work we have set out to do, or work that is adjacent to or that overlaps with our own. Their work might not look exactly like the type of work we do, and those involved may not be our elders, but they are still doing the work. If someone has contributed in any way to the work, acknowledge them. It is imperative to connect with them and uplift their contributions. Seek collaboration and support from them, but also seek to invest and support *their* efforts.

Once you are ready to step into a space with a spirit of gratitude and learning, you will most likely discover who has been leading the work in your community. You might find you encounter resistance. You might feel doubt. Folks may think you are a fraud. I invite you to investigate yourself when this happens. Investigate your intentions. *Are you doing this work for self-recognition or because you truly believe the community is worth investing in?* It is important to not just step into a community believing you know what they are missing or need. Arrive with the intention to learn, while also investing your time and commitment to the process.

So, where exactly do we start? How do we find our elders?

- Make a list of those doing the work you would like to be a part of within a community.
- Find folks who are local and involved in the community in ways you would like to be. Find them by asking others if they know of anyone already doing the work.
- If there is no one doing work in ways you are envisioning, find someone or an organization whose work is adjacent or similar to your vision.
- Do research on the work they've done and learn about them.
- Map-out your plan to connect with these people or organizations. Can you set up a meeting with them? Can you go into their place of business or visit their organization?

Identifying folks and choosing to acknowledge and support them are the easy and fun parts of community building, especially if we lean into uplifting others. We must accept that we are a part of a collective, not alone in our work. We are not saviors. If we have done our research and work in an authentic way, this part will be enjoyable. Learn to support folks already doing the work, even if it seems you are supporting your competition.

After identifying these folks and meeting them, find ways to give them *tu apoyo*. Ask them questions. Be genuine and intentional in what you ask. Attend community forums and events, and support local businesses as a way to encourage and learn what a community truly needs. Sometimes, this means sitting with elders for hours at a time, listening to the stories they have carried for decades. Sometimes, it means receiving admonishment from elders who tell you not to mess things up. Sometimes, it means allowing folks to ask, "Who the hell are you?"

Identifying elders in the community we desire to serve (not to be confused with finding folks who are also doing the work, though both must be done) is the beginning of building your relationship equity. You are investing time into the people and spaces you want to help grow. This builds trust, which is foundational to the next steps in building relationship equity.

As we identify elders or folks we want to acknowledge, we may find our values and principles are challenged. Let these challenges be constructive. We need to allow people to test our intentions because what we're doing will have ripple effects in our community. At these times, we must be sure to know what our values are and why we hold them. If you don't know what those values are, skip to chapter seven, then return to this page.

Building Relationship Equity

Investing in our communities without expecting a return on investment right away works. Doing so is living and thinking with abundance! It is what I love to talk about: relationship equity. Think about building relationship equity as building wealth in a bank account. Now, before we go on, let's be clear about something: while we often operate within communities through *businesses,* in a somewhat transactional way, remember that our community *relationships* are not transactional. For the sake of this discussion on relationship equity, though, we'll use the metaphor of a bank account. Think about how a bank account works: we can't take deposits out of our bank account without investing something into it first. We receive only after we give! As the saying goes, spend money to make money! The question, though, is how do we maintain the integrity of relationships we've invested in? We do so by prioritizing trust. What builds that trust? Leaning into what is sustainable, or what we know we can ALWAYS commit to. When folks know they can depend on you to show up as yourself (authenticity), without hiding anything (transparency) and to follow through and be responsible for your privilege and power (accountability), you will build trust. Authenticity, transparency, and accountability are all crucial to building trust.

> **Building relationships out of TRUST, knowing that you will receive what is meant for you, somehow or in some way, is operating out of abundance.**

Modeling these values is projecting what you desire and expect out of your relationships. Protecting the integrity of those relationships by committing to these values and allowing yourself to be accountable to them is operating out of abundance.

I refer to the process of choosing these values and adhering to them as "leaning in," because it is tricky to do so. It is humbling to continually recommit to the values we wish to shape our lives, relationships, and communities. At times, it is intense. We will be challenged to quit, to reconsider, to dilute our values or our belief systems. Although so many of us desire for communities to shift into strong and connected spaces, we tend to let our values fall to the wayside when our commitment is challenged. And so we must humble ourselves in the interest of healing our communities and bridging generations, and most important of all, leave a legacy of wholeness for those who come after us.

We build relationship equity with elders and honor them at the same time by reaching out to them. Ask for their participation and support. If it is declined, ask why. Ask for their insight. Ask for their blessings. Understand that while they may do things differently than we would, they were born in a different era. And before we can grow intergenerationally, we must be willing to abide by the second golden rule of community building:

GOLDEN RULE OF COMMUNITY BUILDING #2: Respect lived experiences.

In this case, respect our elders' lived experiences. By doing so, we focus on the first tenet of building relationship equity, which is to invest in a relationship by truly believing the person you are in relationship with is the authority on their own lived experiences. This means accepting there is no one better than them to tell their stories. Believe their stories and regard them as true and real. Release the need to judge another's experience and determine the value of it. All lived experiences have value.

Community relationships need all of these components and more. Communities are living, breathing things. They grow and shift with the passing of time and the evolving of the people within them. We must treat our communities and relationships as such: as living, breathing organisms that require care.

Acknowledgement and Gratitude

Let's assume we've established relationships with key players in a community. This doesn't mean we should ignore the work and contributions of other folks in a community who play less visible roles, or whose work goes hand-in-hand with that of key players. We need to acknowledge and show gratitude to those individuals as well. So many people have come before us. How do we honor them and build upon the foundation they have laid for us?

First, we must step outside our pain for a moment, outside our desperation, and look around to truly acknowledge what has been done. Here, we will uncover the identities of those who have been doing the work all along, behind the scenes, building layer upon layer over the foundation for our liberation and healing. These folks have been trading their freedom for progress, keeping their vision, and keeping faith that there would come a time when those willing to carry on would finally arrive.

Then, we lead with gratitude to find our way. Before assuming you are the first to see a need, ask yourself instead, who started the work to meet this need and to whom do we owe gratitude? Assume someone or many people have seen this need and attempted to meet it before we arrived. When we seek to honor their efforts, we come in the spirit of learning, of adding to and growing the work that has already been done.

Be Accountable

Our words are spells. They have power. If we throw our words around carelessly, what are we doing with that power, and are we accountable to it?

> **Prioritizing integrity via following through with our words and actions is an act of accountability. Accountability is as simple as giving our word and abiding by the promises we make.**

Integrity of our words and accountability in our actions are crucial to community building because they protect us from imposing harm and violence on our communities. Being accountable means being committed to truth, honoring one another, and showing up to a conversation or space authentically. It means prioritizing integrity. When we commit to this course of action, we are *practicing* being accountable to our word. These values and practices are interconnected and create a framework for our community work. Within that framework, we build a buffer for ourselves, a space in which we are able to deepen our values of integrity and accountability and foster growth of other values that have positive impacts on our wellbeing.

When we ask for folks to follow through on their word— when we call someone in before we call them out—we are participating in preventative work that keeps moments of harm and violence at bay, in both personal and public spheres. This applies to anyone who desires to invest and co-create within their local communities. We ask them to follow through instead of simply giving people the benefit of the doubt about what they say they have done. We must ask for more than words. We must ask for action. We must ask for proof of lived experience. Giving people the benefit of the doubt is not better than asking for proof of real and lived experience. Proof of lived experience builds and maintains the trust that is so necessary to continue on the path of healing and building. To give context and provide an example of harmful behavior, let me share a personal anecdote I am sure many can relate to:

An individual who attended several of my workshops and events claimed to be committed to and invested in community building within historically excluded and marginalized communities. They said they wanted to highlight Women of Color (WoC) voices and increase access to resources for Women of Color specifically. However, the way in which this person went about their work began to feel harmful to many WoC. Many of these WoC were asked by the individual to speak on behalf of all WoC (as if they could be lumped together) and to speak for very little compensation and/or on behalf of other PoC who were not in the room.

Additionally, this individual complained of PoC not being responsive to their inquiries about complex questions regarding race, equity, and access. This behavior placed the burden of emotional labor on PoC. The final act of harm was this individual's unwillingness to be called-in by the larger historically excluded and marginalized community. Instead of answering the call, they preferred to rely on their smaller group of BIPOC supporters who were not representative of the larger community (who called them in).

In an era where one can Google most questions, listen to a podcast, or read a book, it is inappropriate to ask historically excluded and marginalized people to do emotional labor on your behalf. For many PoC, requests of this nature can feel re-traumatizing. For all of us, it feels negligent and careless. Practicing community building in this way deteriorated trust and gaslit the local BIWOC community by implying the call-in was invalid simply because a select group of staunch supporters, who also happened to be WoC, had said so. This behavior left the larger BIPOC community feeling defensive, concerned, damaged, and doubting their reality. The ripple effect of these actions is still being felt today. Not only did this behavior harm historically excluded and marginalized people on an individual and collective level, it also impaired ongoing and future opportunities for BIPOC to collaborate with allies and supporters. This often occurs when Black or Brown folks lose trust with those who they had understood to be their ally. Black or Brown people working with harmful individuals like this will begin to question an ally's intentions as well. To this day, the individual in question continues to say they desire to center WoC, despite the continuation of their harmful actions.

Demonstrate Commitment

Observing, experiencing. and navigating the damage left in the wake of the previously mentioned individual prompted me to see the value of demonstrating commitment throughout the entire process of building community. I began to understand the third golden rule of community building:

GOLDEN RULE OF COMMUNITY BUILDING #3: Before we can call someone in, that individual must be committed to every step of the community-building process.

Being committed to community building means knowing there are sequential steps to be followed, there is a process that must be adhered to, and the flow and pacing of people's lives must be honored. People do not heal on a timeline, and neither do they grow on one. Our life experiences are not linear. Our approach to community building should reflect all of that.

When damage has been done or violence has been experienced, there may be a call for community organizers and facilitators to prove their commitment to the work and to follow protocol for repairing relationships. This is an opportunity to restore damaged relationships, as well as to learn and grow together.

Commitment, and a disciplined approach to that commitment, can also overturn sabotage when combined. Discipline means getting up after each failure, finding consistency, and refusing to give up. It's important to also understand that lack of discipline and sabotage are two sides of the same coin. At times, we may find ourselves falling back into the mindset of scarcity. When we do so, we start to feel a strong desire to sabotage. Sabotage can look like a lack of commitment, choosing indifference, a lack of follow through, or any behavior that not only forms a barrier to growth but also inhibits or completely derails it. But discipline? Discipline compels us to continue even through the toughest of times. Discipline prods us to recommit over and over again. I believe discipline is the difference between a movement that is short-lived and a movement that transforms into a new way of being.

Listen When You're Called-in

We can hold ourselves accountable by allowing ourselves to be called-in. I believe this is a part of the process we must embrace if we want to be engaged and invested in our communities. Discussing our experiences with call-ins, whether we were called-in or we called someone else in, is vital to moving along conversations about accountability. Rather than shutting down and detaching because of loss or lack of trust (even if that loss or lack is valid) we must identify where and how trust has been lost, then rectify the situation. To heal and build within our communities, we must be able to know what we are asking for and what we need.

Deep below our desires to heal and build within our lives and our communities *con las ganas* to tell a new story. But it is hard to tell a new or different story when we historically excluded and marginalized people are continually told we are not experiencing harm, we are not being targeted, and that White folk do, in fact, have our best interests at heart. In some cases, however, it may not be White folk who are causing harm. It may be our elders, whom we respect and long to be acknowledged by. It may be other PoC whom we feel lack accountability.

The practice of calling in folks and allowing accountability to be a part of the community and relationship-building process is also part of passing on knowledge and building trust. Building relationship equity, trust building, acknowledgement, and honoring the OG's in our community (i.e. our elders) are all parts of practicing accountability and transparency.

Tell a Different Story

When our stories change, when they carry healing and belonging, we gain new power. We gain the power to pass along our lessons, to share the knowledge we have accumulated. We can speak to the patterns and cycles that are no longer serving us as individuals or as a community. We can steer ourselves in a new direction and invest in building sustainable communities.

When we combine belonging and healing, we can begin to tell a different story. We are no longer rehashing the story of what has wounded us or how we have been wronged. We may feel settled, or acquire a sense of peace and clarity. Our story begins to take a different shape, and we are able to share our lessons, highs and lows, without tears in our eyes or those gut-wrenching feelings of bitterness and resentment.

We begin to share this new story of healing, of forgiveness. The tone of our story changes in ways we had never imagined. Somehow, we begin to see the common thread through it all: a sense of belonging. We have a new story to tell. One of commitment, overcoming self-sabotage, and violence. Following through is part of telling a different story. Following through is accountability.

Reflection Prompts

- What feelings did this chapter bring up for you?
- Which parts of this chapter, if any, were hard to read? Why?
- In what ways do you or folks in your culture honor elders?

CHAPTER 3

Recognize Scarcity Mindset & Interrogate Your Intentions

Many times, when we see a lack of trust in our relationships, our communities, and even our businesses, what we are actually seeing is an underlying scarcity mindset and lack of belonging. When we hold a scarcity mindset, we believe there is not enough to go around. Having a scarcity mindset means staying stuck in survival mode, keeping ourselves from stepping onto the path we're meant to follow. A scarcity mindset brings about behavior many refer to as "crabs in a barrel," or everyone scrambling for the same resources and lacking the knowledge and understanding that says, *we are the masters of our destiny, we create our abundance.* A scarcity mindset keeps us from seeing and feeling our power.

When we see patterns of a scarcity mindset and then look at their roots, we find a yearning for belonging and a desire to rest, to not constantly prove ourselves to a world that is watching us, (especially, through the "White gaze"). We can only be subjected to the White gaze by White people. It is the experience of feeling like our historically excluded and marginalized energy is something to be fed on or peered at. The White gaze is distinctly non-engaging and does not facilitate being in relationship with others. As Toni Morrison said, the White gaze is "The little white man that sits on your shoulder and checks out everything you do or say. You sort of knock him off and you're free."

The White gaze considers itself supreme, superior, and the standard. When the White gaze is cast on BIPOC, by default, we are othered. If we constantly feel like we must prove ourselves, we will live in an unending state of lack. There, we will only see that which we do not have or possess. This is a learned pattern of survival that has kept us running for far too long. Living in scarcity keeps us from embracing the rest and joy that comes with abundance and celebration, from finally *disfrutando la vida* we deserve. We deserve to feel the kiss of the sun on our skin and the warmth of our loved ones and their laughter.

I believe that before we can begin to deconstruct our scarcity mindset, we must first identify desires we have not been fulfilling. Often, those are our primal needs and desires for belonging. Belonging is the inexplicable urge to lay one's burden down and rest, to just be. Showing up this way is showing up as our authentic selves. It is perhaps one of the most joyous experiences we can have in life. There is relief in this experience. Yet, showing up authentically will be different for each of us. It can mean showing up in the strength we never embraced as individuals and with the uniqueness of our ideas (a.k.a. our magic sauce). It can mean understanding our unique value. It can mean saying what we mean to say, not what we think someone wants to hear. It is being truthful about who we are.

Showing up authentically always means being vulnerable. Being vulnerable is not the same as being weak. In actuality, being vulnerable is powerful in that it liberates us and encourages and allows others to do the same. Showing up authentically is also a practice.

It is daring to show the world who we really are.

It is sharing our shortcomings and our strengths.

It is refusing to code switch.

I believe showing up authentically is showing up as our *whole* selves. For example, in February 2022, I hosted a gathering for the non-profit I founded, The Tacoma Women of Color Collective. I was exhausted on the night of the event and had already attended several functions earlier in the day. The thought of leaving my children at home, again, for another event, broke my heart. So I packed up my kids and took them with me even though I would likely need to speak in front of a large crowd. I accepted that I would probably do so with both my children in tow. That is exactly what I did.

The turnout for the event was wonderful and beyond my expectations. But more importantly, it was what I had envisioned at the beginning of my journey building the Tacoma Women of Color Collective: I was participating in building community and growing relationships based on our shared experiences. I shed tears on stage while holding my seven-month-old daughter and watching my son sitting at a small table across the room. I didn't care that I was crying in front of everyone. In fact, that is exactly who I am, who I MUST be. I can't be anything else, or anyone else, any longer. I can't be any smaller, or quieter, or less messy. This is authenticity. It is showing up with the parts of ourselves that we know we can no longer repress or hold back and sharing them with others.

When we share our true selves and our stories, others are able to see themselves reflected in us. Sharing our authentic selves gives silent permission to those around us to do the same. It says, *if I can do it, so can you.* Showing up authentically is a pillar in the room of belonging and abundance. Remember, there is no abundance without authenticity. Showing up authentically is crucial because it helps to create the framework for sustainable community-building practices. That framework is built on four key pillars:

- **Authenticity:** Showing up as we are, which gives others permission to do the same.
- **Transparency:** Being honest with oneself and with others, lowering the walls that normally keep us from connecting in our humanity with one another. Transparency builds trust.
- **Accountability:** Being responsible for commitments we have made. Accountability is honoring our word. This is critical to building lasting relationships.
- **Sustainability:** Focusing on present needs while investing in the future.

This framework is the vehicle to restoring our communities and moving from scarcity to abundance. Let's take a look at each of these values as they relate to moving from scarcity to abundance.

Authenticity

When you show up as you are, others feel they can do the same. Showing up authentically **shifts the energy in the room to create space for what is *real*.** We signal to others that we bring empathy, compassion, a desire to understand, and most importantly, safety, to a shared space.

Transparency

Transparency is what allows us to show our humanity and connect within that humanity. Transparency says, "No, I don't have it all together, but I am giving it my best shot today." It says, "Wow, I see I hurt you. I see I am biased or have stereotyped you, and I acknowledge my mistakes in doing so." Transparency is acknowledging the humanity of our experiences and allowing it to connect us. It is showing up in honesty, rather than obscuring the truth of our experiences. It is saying, "We are here to get it right, not to be right," as Brene Brown teaches us.

Protecting ourselves with transparency is vetting those around us to ensure they are present for the right reasons and that they are meeting us honestly. Protecting ourselves through our own transparency and through requiring it from others is essential.

Transparency also allows others to relate with us. It allows them to see into our (usually) unspoken or private journeys in life, and into our thought processes. When that happens, more often than not, they say, *Oh, me too!* Our transparency shows others they are not alone and that in spite of our successful or tough exteriors, we also struggle, we also submit to the full human experience.

Transparency allows trust to be built. Being transparent means telling the truth of our experiences and allowing it to connect us with others. As a personal example, I often forget or fail to share that I received a GED instead of a high school diploma. While that may not seem like a big deal at first, it is important to say aloud because it allows others to see themselves reflected in me when they otherwise wouldn't. Folks often automatically assume I had an easy, relatively painless path to my current standing in the world. But when I share that I did not complete high school and received a GED instead, and that I had to fight tooth and nail to enter into a community college because my parents were so behind on their taxes they couldn't apply to FAFSA on my behalf, folks begin to see my humanity. Transparency and building trust are crucial for enabling ourselves to lower our walls and come out of a survival mindset to rest.

Accountability

Accountability requires integrity, which is critical to building lasting relationships. Accountability paves the path to success and change in community building because it gives folks something they can count on. It builds upon authenticity and transparency and says, "We will do what we said we are going to do. We are responsible for our words, actions, and commitments." Without accountability for our words and our actions to each other, we simply start, struggle, then stop in our tracks, never truly fulfilling our word or purpose.

Accountability holds all the other pieces of community building together. It calls us to take action based on our words, to move past our feelings and into long-term commitment to building community, and to lean into discomfort and accountability. It calls us to not only account for the beautiful parts of our journey, but also the harm we might impose on others.

Accountability is directly tied to earning the public's trust. Read *public* as *community*. If there are no methods or practice of accountability within an organization, company, or even within an individual's personal practice of building community or being in relationship with others, trust will be lost. And trust is a foundational part of engaging historically excluded and marginalized communities. How do we build trust? By becoming people of our word.

Authenticity, transparency, and accountability combined become the vehicle to restoring our communities and moving from scarcity to abundance. They are the vital components of sustainability and an abundance mindset. Only with sustainability can we focus on present needs while investing in the future.

Sustainability

Sustainability is consistently investing our energy and work into present needs rather than pretending they don't exist, which helps us arrive at our intended destination. Now, if we continue to think about the equity held in our community relationships, we will find our equity can increase through consistently investing in the current moment with an eye toward the hopes and visions for our future as a collective. Often, folks tend to lose sight of the value of investing in others via showing up to their events, buying their books, sending a donation, or simply sharing their business or recommending a person through word of mouth. Investing in folks and organizations in a real way that centers building relationships over being transactional is key to authentic community building. This is paramount to success. Doing so reminds us that we are shooting for more than just healing our own present wounds. We are also laying a foundation for those who come after us.

> **Sustainability teaches us how to build the foundation for our legacy. It requires commitment.**
>
> **Commitment builds trust with community organizers, agencies, organizations, and the communities they serve.**
>
> **And there is no community without trust.**
>
> **There is no healing without trust.**

I have treated these four values as pillars in my approach to community building and have seen a significant change in the way myself and others collectively identify and understand the gaps within our community-building frameworks because of them. If we can become personally invested in this work and recognize the connection between our microcosms (homes and families) and our macrocosms (communities and larger groups we are a part of), we can begin to truly understand that we are not alone in what we experience;

that our communities reflect what is happening in our homes, and vice versa; and that it is crucial to recommit to the principles and values we identify as necessary to sustain the restoration of our communities.

I have found that my role in community building is to facilitate, or guide the process of, unearthing our most cherished values. It is to encourage folks to become principled enough to not only stand by those values, but carry them out in building the relationships and communities they long for. We can simultaneously build out our own personal framework of abundance while also focusing on abundance within our communities. When I say abundance, I think of a lush, abundant garden filled with joy. I want to live in that garden.

I want to uproot the weeds of scarcity mindset, impostor syndrome, and trauma response in my garden and plant joy in their places.

I want to cultivate more time for connection, community, and belonging.

To cultivate in a garden of abundance, we must uproot:

- **The Scarcity Mindset**, which tells us there is not enough to go around. This mindset is born out of generations of survival and leads us to believe all resources are scarce.

- **Imposter Syndrome**, or the notion that we aren't enough and don't deserve to be in certain spaces.
- **The Trauma Response**, or our drive to overperform, overprepare, and prove ourselves because we have been underestimated, undervalued, and underrepresented for so long.[1]

Acknowledge that this process often feels like being caught in a loop, one in which we don't know where the scarcity mindset, imposter syndrome, and trauma response start or end. These principles of scarcity are all connected to a lack of belonging, rejection, and performative behavior, while abundance is connected to belonging, acceptance, and showing up as our authentic selves. Lean into these moments of unease and evaluate them with as much objectivity as possible. Trace the roots of what you're feeling so you can find *their* roots. Investigate any moments of not belonging that spring up for you as well as how you feel when you experience

1 When I say "trauma response," I am referring to our reactions to generations and years of gaslighting, racism, oppression, marginalization, and disenfranchisement. I am referring to the impact of the systems and actions which ultimately are meant to undermine us. We carry an invisible burden due to these experiences. We must choose to transform that burden (perhaps manifested in our anger and frustration regarding a lack of recognition and/or being bypassed) into abundance by honoring, acknowledging, and affirming ourselves in our present state. We are works in progress. We must find balance by breaking the momentum of overworking and proving our worth.

the opposite. Consider how they're connected and know you are not alone in this experience.

Commitment to Timely Integration

Commitment to timely integration is a quantifiable language that communicates specific BIPOC needs. More simply put, it is building trust. But "building trust" doesn't sound professional. It doesn't call anyone to action. And no one outside of historically excluded and marginalized communities truly cares about garnering the trust of our people. Because of this, I often use "commitment to timely integration" as a replacement for "feedback that builds trust" in my work as a consultant. This highlights the disconnect in the language we use surrounding relationship and community building and our actions.

When we call for commitment to timely integration, we are calling for holding people, institutions, and organizations accountable. We are asking them to commit to integrating our feedback in a timely manner. Our feedback should be integrated into the process of community building, serving the community, and building relationships. Authentic relationships cannot be built within our communities without the opportunity for feedback *and* the commitment to integrate that feedback into renewed processes and approaches. We can add all that information to evaluations of someone's performance or work. This evaluation can be done by the people, organizations, companies, or agencies involved. It can also become a requirement by which someone must remain committed before being selected for the responsibility of serving the community. Because what is community building without the voices and feedback of the most marginalized amongst us? It is gatekeeping. It is simply the retaining of power and privilege.

To integrate change we must be willing to take the feedback, or whatever catalysts for positive change we've experienced, and integrate them into our work. When we decide to be community organizers or activists, or simply contributing members of our community, part of our own accountability to the group is integrating change. But what does that look like in practice? It looks like not paying lip service (all talk, no action), being genuinely open to feedback, and being committed to the implementation of the feedback someone brings to us. It also means reflecting on that feedback and doing internal work to understand its implications. Doing so builds trust. When an individual or an organization does not engage in rather quick implementation of feedback, trust is lost and walls are built.

This is not glamorous work. Admitting our shortcomings, or areas in need of change, is not easy. Being targeted as the receiver of all issues, big and small, within our communities is no small burden. And that's *before* we even commit to taking action, or integrating feedback, following through, or holding space for nuanced solutions. As an example, let's look at accessibility. Accessibility, at a community function, for instance, requires dialogue to be translated into multiple languages, verbally and on printed material. Providing accessibility also means ensuring content is written in a way that ensures most folks in the room can understand its message and does not exceed general reading comprehension levels. But we might not know any of those actions are necessary unless we listen to feedback from others.

This is all hard but necessary work. In fact, our communities won't survive without it. Understand that feedback in one area, whether positive or negative, does not mean we are failing or excelling in all areas. We must hold an openness and awareness for continual growth instead, while solidifying foundational components.

Reflection Prompts

- Where have you identified the scarcity mindset, imposter syndrome, or trauma response showing up in your individual work?

- Are you or the organization you are a part of committed to timely integration, or integrating feedback from the communities you serve? If so, how does this shift the work that you do within your community? If not, how has that posed a barrier to growth?

CHAPTER 4

Breaking Bread

> **"Rarely, if ever, are any of us healed in isolation. Healing is an act of communion."**
>
> **— bell hooks**

As we discuss what it means to honor work that was carried out before us and to support work being done in the present, I invite us to consider the power of breaking bread with one another, both literally and figuratively.

To break bread with one another is to set aside our differences and to step into shared experiences of communion, nourishing ourselves and each other.

In this context, breaking bread means facilitating conversation between groups and individuals and choosing to come together in a communal way to begin or restore relationships. Breaking bread is inviting community-oriented folks to lower their walls and lean into the synergy that occurs between varying points of expertise and aligned desires, all in efforts to uplift and restore communities.

The act of breaking bread removes barriers that typically exist between folks because of age, knowledge, academic expertise, or other factors, and serves to highlight the differences between us that enrich our lives. We're talking about cultural differences, nuances, understandings, and individual wants and desires. We can weave a beautiful pattern that incorporates both our commonalities and differences within the tapestries of our communities.

Breaking bread will reveal our strengths and areas of opportunity for connection, as well. Though we may feel like we are moving on, collectively, from the fragmentedness in our communities, there will always be folks who remain stuck, feeling as if their needs aren't being met or have been overlooked. This is a very real element of community building. Folks who feel like they aren't getting their needs met in the community are still a part of that community's fabric and we, as participants, must acknowledge them.

Although it is painful, and at times the reasoning may not be clear, we must also lean into the folks who are not, for whatever reason, able to join us in breaking bread. Who are the folks who refuse to break bread with us? Perhaps they are those who feel left out or not represented. Perhaps they feel they've been hurt by others in our community or feel disconnected and unable to reconnect. Regardless, if we are to assume the responsibility of building community, it is important to consider these folks, engage with them, and genuinely care about their voices being integrated into feedback and change. We must consider these people or groups, regardless of how we might feel about them.

Once we are at the table, we must also ask, *What do we do when it gets uncomfortable*? The answer is that we must hold space for uncertainty and constructive conversation. We can invite a trusted community member to mediate the space. Whatever we do, we should not ignore the discomfort. Instead, create a space where the discomfort can be expressed, where it can breathe and find comfort in acknowledgment. This is why commiting to openness and integration of feedback is essential.

Regardless of whether or not we are able to integrate feedback in a way that our community members or stakeholders desire, it is important to allow critical feedback, and sometimes unfounded feedback, to have space, as well. Allowing feedback in, even if seemingly unfounded, allows for the refining of our community building, our community healing and integration, a check on our intentions, and conveying the message that we are committed to our community and the work, no matter how uncomfortable things may get. We must be able to stay committed to our work even when we find ourselves up against conflict. Leaning into humanity, vulnerability, and the unknowingness of it all, is what connects us as a community and facilitates healing, if we allow it.

I understand that age, positionality, and intersectionality all impact the lens from which we view these experiences. Even though some lenses may not be a part of our specific identity or experience, they will still have a significant impact on the community-building experience. Yet, if we can sit down and break bread, even for a moment, we can transform barriers into bridges leading to knowledge, experience, insight, and perspectives that we wouldn't otherwise be able to cross. We can never walk in someone else's shoes, but we can hold space for them, fill that space with acceptance, value their lived experiences, and acknowledge them. Doing so gives life and power to people. It places an agreed-upon value on each and every individual experience.

Honoring our Elders

As part of the acknowledgement of lived experience, we must honor our elders. It is crucial to acknowledge our elders, or those who have come before us, because they may be in a phase of their life in which they want to contribute to their communities and future generations. This phase of life is sometimes called generativity (as opposed to stagnation). The term "generativity" was coined by ego psychologist Erik Erikson. Erikson theorizes that folks in this stage of life, usually at middle age (forty to sixty-five years old), face the choice of living in generativity vs. stagnation. Generativity means they have "left their mark," and have impacted the world around them via personal contribution. Contributions can happen via programs, mentorship, or building deep and lasting relationships with family or friends. Stagnation, on the other hand, occurs when someone feels they have not made their mark on the world or impacted generations who come after them; they feel stagnant. A simple example is mentorship. A person within this age group, reflecting back on their life and their contributions and engaging in mentorship with younger folks is in generativity. A person who has failed to find a way to contribute to others or their community, or who did not heed the call to mentor others in their life, is in stagnation.

The effects of generativity and stagnation have been found to be linked to overall health, manifesting themselves physically and mentally. There is an improvement in health due to generativity, which can present as productivity, having deep and meaningful relationships, and feeling deep fulfillment.

We explore what it means to live in this phase of life for a few reasons. Firstly, we are all human and as long as we live, there is a high likelihood we will face certain existential experiences, like generativity. Secondly, understanding where a person may be coming from (their lived experience) allows us to open up to them in ways that perhaps we had not been able to before. With this in mind, let's revisit what it means to honor our elders in the context of receiving feedback.

In order to be oriented in the most productive direction, and to not have to start from scratch, I encourage you to sit with your elders. Allow their stories to fill and guide you. Allow them to challenge you. Allow your layers of guardedness, uncertainty, pain, and misunderstanding to fall away so you can sit with the intention to hear, acknowledge, and see.

Additionally, allow for constructive criticism to become commonplace. Doing so ensures we do not startle every time we hear it. And because we have been leaning into both the light and dark of our journey—the easy and the tough parts, the beautiful and the ugly aspects—critics and criticism will not come as a total surprise to us. And even if it does, we can embrace it and allow it to visit us. Give it room to teach us what we need to know, and then release it. Constructive criticism often startles us when we receive it, especially from our best supporters and most loyal fans. Yes, they love what we do and who we are, but they also see where we can grow. An individual or group of people committed to us enough to offer constructive criticism is a dazzling gem. Folks who do not care, who are apathetic to us, would never bother to offer such insight or assistance. At times, we get surprised or alarmed because we have received so many *yeses* that we forgot there would be *nos*, as well. But hearing *no* can push us to do better. We need these *nos* to grow! When feedback startles us, we must embrace it, heed it lightly, and examine the different parts of it before we let it go.

Let's talk about why we need feedback at all. And why should we break bread? Why do we need our elders? The answer is clear: because we are greater than the sum of our parts. We are greater than just our individual experiences. Yes, we are powerful alone. But together, collectively, we are unstoppable. Together, if we honor one another, lean into discomfort and embrace uncertainty, we can progress and move further and in ways we might never have imagined. This is synergy.

> **Synergy is the interaction or cooperation of two or more organizations, substances, or other agents to produce a combined effect greater than the sum of their separate effects.**

Reflection Prompts

- What is your biggest barrier, individually or in community, to breaking bread?
- What does breaking bread mean for you?

CHAPTER 5

Learn the Power of Leveraging, Collaboration, & Amplification

Collaboration is believing the combined efforts of a group of individuals is greater than the sum of its parts. It is believing we each have our own part to play and that together, we can have more impact than we would alone.

Leveraging one another is knowing we may not be able to shine in one space, but by playing to each other's strengths in various spaces, we can each stand where we are strongest. Essentially, leveraging is doing what we are each good at and asking others to step in where they are most skilled. Leveraging one another in our strengths and trusting in collaboration is believing someone else's work is just as valuable as ours and may serve part of a larger mission. Not every individual must carry the weight of the collective. Each individual can rest knowing that if they are authentic in their part, transparent in their process, and practiced and accountable to the mission, they will suss out the work in a way that is lasting and sustainable. We must leverage one another's skills and talents to thrive.

Amplifying one another is knowing and understanding that the intersections we each live at may give us some level of privilege and power, and that it is our duty to leverage that power and privilege to raise up those who exist with less. Amplification is lending a megaphone, either earned or given to you, to another's voice, cause, or mission. It is using your own platform, network, and connections to increase someone else's reach. It is sharing someone's name in support of their work in a room, or sharing it with a person who may never have accessed it otherwise.

Sometimes I find that folks become so frustrated by the disconnect they see in their communities that they decide they are the only person doing work and/or the only person qualified to do the work, fill a role, or address an issue. They don't check-in to see who's already doing the work. They don't break bread. And they certainly don't collaborate, leverage, or amplify one another. Why not? Perhaps because the survival mindset has won over in their psyche. Or maybe they have a lack of understanding surrounding the idea that some folks may just be focused on doing their individual part (which is exactly what we need them to do). We do not need anyone doing something that isn't authentic to who they are.

What we need is for folks to let go of their frustrations and fears. We need to find a way to lean into the work even when we are scared or uncomfortable. We need to challenge the distrust and scarcity we have been operating out of. While in survival or scarcity mindsets, we find it hard to believe there's enough for all of us. It is hard to believe there is a world outside of the one we've been operating in. We get so stuck in a survival mindset that we start to believe there is not enough of anything to go around. This reinforces the survival mindset and pushes us to choose silence over the amplification of others. Consequently, we do not offer our platforms, nor do we suggest partnerships or collaborations with others. In this way, steps or pieces of the community-building process are consistently skipped over in the formation and foundational stages of community-building efforts. The ritual of honoring those who came before us, and those who are doing the work, goes undone. The practice of breaking bread with one another gets omitted. Coming to community members in humility, to request their knowledge, guidance, and blessing, is lost.

We also need folks to let go of performative behavior. Yes, performative behavior is more comfortable than choosing authenticity, transparency, and accountability. It's easier to be friendly with people and act like best friends in public than it is to be authentic. But when we show up this way, performing instead of engaging, it's much harder to address our differences one-on-one or to take the chance of collaborating and partnering with others. And when things get tough, it's harder to show up in an authentic way and to choose transparency. It's even more challenging to respond to a call-in.

A call-in can look like folks inquiring about following up our words with actions. A call-in can look like people sharing ways in which our behavior has harmed them. A call-in can be folks sharing that the groups whose perspectives are crucial to a community and/or are being represented in a conversation are being left out of the conversation altogether. And that is unacceptable. A call-in may be folks reminding us of the power and privilege we hold.

A call-in is *usually* an ask to consider more critical thinking and acknowledgment of the complexity of an issue. I urge you, if you have been called-in or are experiencing any of these situations, please answer the call. Answer before you are called out.

> **We can talk until we're blue in the face about community building, but what is actually revolutionary is putting the changes we want to see into daily practice.**

I want to marry revolution with these practices, but right now, it feels like no one else wants that. I want to revolutionize our community spaces and the traditional ways in which we approach leadership and culture (both our own and the collective culture). I want to revolutionize these spaces because when I look around, I see so much richness in us. I see the answers to all the issues we face, to the individual and collective healing and strength we are all hoping for. I see the answers to the brokenness we are experiencing in our communities and which we desire to change. But when this brokenness is confronted with discipline and accountability, I see folks fall off. Their commitment crumbles. Many people want to gloss over and skimp on the daily practice of revolutionizing, which to me, is a dedication to authenticity, transparency, and accountability.

I want to see revolutionizing become something we practice every day, something we commit to and stand by. I want to see us be committed to the dismantling of systems, traditions, and ways of life that have never served us. We must become disciplined in our approach and understand that this shift in mindset, from scarcity to abundance, will carry us all the way through not having enough to having more than we ever dreamed of. And I truly believe we can do this together.

So, what does it mean to "do it right?" It means committing to practicing that which we actually wish existed in our lives and communities. It means practicing showing up authentically. It means practicing transparency. It means leaning into the process of learning and developing as a collective. It means practicing grace.

We must commit to abundance and not scarcity. We must examine our own intentions, privilege, and power regularly. We must accept that this process takes time. Nothing happens overnight, especially collective change. We are only one piece of a whole. As such, we must commit to self-evaluation and embracing feedback. Part of our journey to healing within community includes being open to growth and understanding that the uncertainty about the journey is part of the process, and the process takes a lifetime.

There is no peace in revolution.
There is no peace in change.
The fire keeps us awake through the night,
Lighting every nook and cranny.
We are full of thoughts and desires,
Full of dreams deferred.
Change rocks us like a boat at sea.
Water begins to fill holes,
We feel like we are sinking, drowning.
Then, survival rises up in our throats.
We feel as if we are choking on our desire to live.
There is no peace in change.
There is no peace in revolution.
But peace will come.
But the work must be done.
Water must be dumped out.
Holes must be patched.
The body must drink and rest.
Then peace can come.
Then the sea can calm.
The sun can shine and dry-up memories of the storm.
The memories will float away.
Let them go.

Reflection Prompts

- Reflect on the content of this chapter. How does it make you feel and what does it bring to mind?
- What might resistance to these ideas look like in practice?
- What is it about leveraging or amplifying others and their work that feels difficult to practice?

CHAPTER 6

What Are You Committed to?

I've questioned the need for and validity of this book many, many times throughout its unfolding. I've questioned whether or not the values and processes I've outlined, the framework for sustainability of authenticity, transparency, and accountability, are too much. Is it too much to ask myself and others to live up to these values? Is challenging ourselves to honor our elders and break bread with one another realistic? Does anyone do that anymore? Does anyone want to? Are my methods universal enough for folks to use in spaces in which they desire to build community?

By questioning the content within this book, I realized I was questioning myself. This content has been living within me my entire life. I've been sharing Instagram posts, workshops, presentations, trainings, and one-on-one consulting sessions for years now. I've been holding it, living with it, sharing it, and repeating it. And much of what is written here are parts of myself and my practice that I decided were too ugly or impractical to share with others along the way. Yet these are the exact pieces of myself, of all of us, which become the processes we utilize to make our visions realities.

Once I realized I was questioning myself, I understood that this was my ultimate challenge: to not run from vulnerability. I've been sharing just enough to get by for years. I've been holding the softest fruit of my heart back all this time. Long ago, I decided the risk of sharing it was too great for me to bear. *What would everyone say? What critiques and laughter would follow? Who am I to speak as an expert about any of this?*

As I explored the fear and criticism I thought might come from people I trust or strangers, I found that no outside voices were harsher than the criticism perpetuated within the walls of my own mind. My self-talk had beaten me down so fiercely that it had skewed my perspective of my own desires, vision, and achievements.

Yet here I am. And here is this book, a beautiful dove I offer to the world.

In Guadalajara, a city in Jalisco, Mexico, it is common to own doves or other entrancing birds. They're often kept in cages on rooftops, where they eye the city day and night, observing and learning under blue and black skies but rarely living outside their cages. The ideas in this book are just like these caged birds. I have kept them behind lock and key, in cages on the roof of my house, allowing them to breathe air, see clear skies, but remain confined for fear of what they might do. They might fly away if I let them out! They might love freedom so much they never come back. They may embarrass me by pooping on a visitor's head! They might look at me with sadness in their eyes once they realize all they have been missing. Those imagined looks… I cannot live with them. I cannot be responsible for keeping these ideas, this book, caged. I must let them go and let them be free. My ideas must fly, soar, and feel the wind beneath them. It's time.

Now, I return to my original questions: does anyone want to honor elders and break bread with one another? Are my methods universal enough for folks to use in the spaces they desire to build community? I think the answers are yes and no. For those who desire to dig deeper and build in a way they never have before, these methods are applicable and accessible. I also believe that if someone only wants to scratch the surface of a community's needs, and say they took the necessary steps to move and build community without actually doing so, this content will feel like too much of an ask, as it requires one to reflect upon themselves, then choose a kind of vulnerability many are not used to bearing in community. To those folks, I say, *lean in.* Lean into the possibility that exists by daring to commit to people, relationships, and building community. Live in a way that perhaps you never have before. Understand that in order to have new and different *outcomes*, we must have new and different *inputs*. Understand that the account of strong community values, an account we desire to see full, does not become full on its own. It is dependent on the level of investment we are willing to give.

Leave the camp of people who speak performatively, who complain about and criticize issues in our communities, who make hollow verbal commitments to changing and healing us. There is no substance or action behind their words. Yet only action behind the words that shape our dreams and visions can breathe life into those dreams and visions. Our actions demonstrate our commitment. Our commitment is made up of our values and principles. Those values, in turn, transform our thoughts into action, once again. It is a cycle. Taking action is practicing new ways of being that radically shift old systems. Through this action, we find the magic of healing and change. It is here, in the embracing of the discomfort and the leaning into internal work, the shadow work, the difficult parts, where we begin to fill our accounts.

The processes I outline for moving from scarcity to abundance require us to lean into discomfort in a way that many of us perhaps have never experienced before, whether alone in our own thoughts or in community. These processes ask us to hear the call-ins; to do work and research who has been doing that same or similar work; to find ways to honor them. These processes ask us to sit through admonishment that perhaps we've been too thin-skinned to sit through before. These processes ask us to build an account of trust and integrity, made possible by regular deposits of authenticity, transparency, and accountability. These values, when put into practice, encourage us to reimagine and unearth the roots of our communities that have been buried by pain, hurt, betrayal, oppression, and survival. They remind us that operating out of scarcity, or behaving like crabs in a barrel, is no longer our story. We can choose to put into practice that which we desire to hold most dear within our communities.

We desire everyone to show up as they are, in authenticity.

We desire the ability to be honest and real, in transparency.

We desire to be people of our word, both to ourselves and one another, in accountability.

We desire to build intergenerationally by honoring our elders, youth, and children.

We desire to build together and collaborate by learning who is already investing in our communities.

We desire to break bread and embrace the synergy that is sure to exist when we all sit down at the table.

I invite you to reimagine with me.

I invite you to unearth the longings within yourself, the yearning to belong, the subtle yet persistent desire to heal.

I invite you to consider what it can mean for us, especially as historically excluded and marginalized people, to lean into community using the philosophies I've presented in this book.

I welcome you to join me on this path of healing, individually and collectively, in community.

EPILOGUE

Legacy

I believe that when we truly grasp the multiplicity of our existence, we begin to see the weight of our choices much differently. We begin to see how imperative it is to live with intent. When we begin to see that *we are our ancestors*, while also being ourselves, and that we carry generations to come within us, we begin to see the importance of legacy. We begin to see that it has never been about just us. It has always been about those who have come before us, those who walk with us now, and those who will come after us. We were once like those who will come after us. And one day, we will be those who came before us.

But we must ask, how did we leave the account? Did we withdraw it into deficit? Or did we invest into it with the intent to build generational wealth? What is generational wealth in the context of community? I believe generational wealth in a community begins with a foundation of healing. I believe that generational wealth is cultivating spaces of belonging and healing, spaces where we can be our truest selves. And then, generational wealth can show up as collaboration.

We cannot lean into our most powerful work when we allow our accounts to overdraft. Allowing this to happen is allowing the survival mindset to continue and being complicit in its perpetuation. Overdrafting our accounts can show up as allowing ourselves to return to scarcity after living in abundance. It can mean stepping out of authenticity and transparency into a more superficial and people-pleasing space. It can mean demanding of others what we are not willing to do ourselves. It can mean making assumptions about our communities without doing our research or making investments.

To continually maintain our personal selves or accounts, and those of our communities, we must be willing to create a legacy of healing, commitment, doing shadow work, and practicing the framework for sustainability. We must change the way we look at community, how we belong to it, and how we show up, by not thinking of it as a destination, but as a daily practice. Just as we must choose ourselves, reflect, and do our internal work daily, we must understand the ebb and flow of being in community as similar. And just as in our daily practice, we do not move from scarcity to abundance linearly, nor cultivate community that way. Just as we live and breathe, grow and change, so do our communities. We must learn to embrace the concept of putting into daily practice that which we wish to see in ourselves and our communities. There is no quick fix for anything. Everything requires commitment, time, grace, and love.

APPENDIX A

Glossary

Amplifying: Lending our platform or privilege to give more power, reach, and impact to the voices of historically excluded and marginalized folks.

BIPOC: Black and Indigenous People of Color

BIWOC: Black and Indigenous Women of Color

Community: The group(s) of people we share experiences with. Those who we build with, based on a shared vision of family, interconnectedness, and what we wish to see around us locally.

Gaslighting: Being told our reality is not true or real, therefore making us question our life experiences and/or reality.

Generativity: "Making our mark" on the world by caring for others, as well as through creating and accomplishing feats that make the world a better place.

Healing: Returning to softness, releasing our pain, and surrendering to love and belonging.

Imposter Syndrome: Believing we are frauds and/or not capable of the work we do; feeling as if we will be "found out" for not being up to par.

Leveraging: Using our power and privilege to shift power and attention toward folks with the necessary skill set or services to see something through.

Relationship Equity: Investing in our relationships and building up an account within our relationships.

Scarcity Mindset: Believing there is not enough to go around. Often compared to behaving like crabs in a barrel.

Synergy: The interaction or cooperation of two or more organizations, substances, or similar agents to produce a combined effect greater than the sum of their separate effects.

Trauma Response: Our drive to overperform, overprepare, and prove ourselves because we have been underestimated, undervalued, and underrepresented for so long.

White Gaze: The experience of feeling like our historically excluded and marginalized energy is something to be fed on or peered at. The White gaze is distinctly non-engaging and does not facilitate being in relationship with others. The White gaze considers itself supreme, superior, and the standard.

APPENDIX B

Golden Rules of Community Building

#1: Never, and I mean *never*, assume you know what a community needs better than those within it.

#2: Respect lived experiences.

#3: Before we can call someone in, that individual must be committed to every step of the community building process.

Acknowledgements

I want to acknowledge the integral role my spiritual journey and ancestors played in writing this book. Tapping into my intuition and ancestral wisdom made this book possible. I have deep gratitude for the spiritual and metaphysical components of my life-journey.

I also want to thank my son, Romelo. Even at only four years old, Romelo has shown me the breadth of possibilities that exist for humans if we show up with love and authenticity. I am also grateful for the experience of being pregnant with my second child, Citlali, and our post-partum experience, both of which coincided with putting this book together. I wrote most of this book within our first six months together and I can't help but believe the vulnerability and words I was able to access were partly because of her presence.

Lastly, I'd like to thank my community, my family, my friends, the Tacoma Women of Color Collective, Blue Cactus Press and everyone who allowed me to flesh-out my reimagining of healing and being in community. Thank you.

About the Author

Krista R. Pérez aims to share her story, all parts of her story, including her softest and strongest parts, her sacred nature, the joy of motherhood, and her deeply rooted cultural values, to create spaces for Women of Color to show up in all capacities. Krista is also a proponent of integrated leadership, in which we bring all parts of ourselves to our professional workspaces. By making our whole selves visible we learn to value our whole selves, and others, as mothers and community members.

Krista's focus and work is anchored in centering anti-racist, equitable and community centered work. Her multi-disciplinary perspective allows her to view her work through several lenses, which include her identity as a second generation immigrant and descendant of a migrant working family, her undergraduate degree in law, economics, and public policy, small business/entrepreneurial knowledge and experience, and her dedication to community organizing. These experiences inform the work Krista has done as president and founder of the nonprofit organization, the Tacoma Women of Color Collective; co-founder of The Community Market, a PoC centered market; and Perez Consulting, a diversity, equity, accessibility and inclusion consulting business.

At Perez Consulting, authenticity, transparency and accountability are prioritized. Krista believes it is important to uproot anti-Black, racist, ableist, and biased values while amplifying the voices of communities of color. Key to this is creating safe spaces for Black, Indigenous and People of Color and striving for equitable outcomes.

Unearthing Our Roots
By Krista R. Pérez

ISBN 978-1-7368209-6-4

First Edition
Editing by Christina Vega, Nisha Bolsey, & Kate Threat
Cover Design & Layout by Knic Pfost

This book was partially funded by the Tacoma Arts Commission, which supports Tacoma's community by funding local artists and arts organizations, providing technical assistance organizing Tacoma's annual Art at Work month, and oversees the public art program.

Blue Cactus Press
Tacoma Washington
bluecactuspress.com